First World War
and Army of Occupation
War Diary
France, Belgium and Germany

14 DIVISION
Divisional Troops
Loyal North Lancashire Regiment
15th Battalion Pioneers
1 June 1918 - 15 June 1919

WO95/1890/6

The Naval & Military Press Ltd
www.nmarchive.com
Published in association with The National Archives

Published by

The Naval & Military Press Ltd

Unit 10 Ridgewood Industrial Park,

Uckfield, East Sussex,

TN22 5QE England

Tel: +44 (0) 1825 749494

www.naval-military-press.com

www.nmarchive.com

This diary has been reprinted in facsimile from the original. Any imperfections are inevitably reproduced and the quality may fall short of modern type and cartographic standards.

© **Crown Copyright**
Images reproduced by permission of The National Archives, London, England, 2015.

Contents

Document type	Place/Title	Date From	Date To
Heading	WO95/1890/6		
Heading	14th Division 15th Bn Loyal Nth Lancashire (Pioneer Bn) Jun 1918-Jun 1919 To France 1918 June		
Heading	War Diary 15th Bn. Loyal North Lancs Regt. (Pioneers) From June 17th 1918 To June 30th 1918 Volume i		
War Diary	Torcy	01/06/1918	14/06/1918
War Diary	La Goulee	15/06/1918	15/06/1918
War Diary	Boulogne	16/06/1918	16/06/1918
War Diary	Bullswater Camp. Surrey	17/06/1918	30/06/1918
Heading	War Diary 15th Bn. Loyal North Lancs Regt. (Pioneers) From July 1st 1918 To July 31st 1918 Vol II		
War Diary	Bullswater Camp	01/07/1918	01/07/1918
War Diary	Pirbright	02/07/1918	04/07/1918
War Diary	Ostrohove	05/07/1918	05/07/1918
War Diary	Bologne	06/07/1918	06/07/1918
War Diary	Regertinghe	07/07/1918	11/07/1918
War Diary	Herbinghem	12/07/1918	12/07/1918
War Diary	Mentque	13/07/1918	31/07/1918
Heading	War Diary 15th Bn Loyal N. Lancs Regt (Pioneers) From August 1st 1918 To August 31st 1918 Vol 3		
War Diary	Mentque	01/08/1918	17/08/1918
War Diary	Le Marais 27 a/R 2 a	18/08/1918	19/08/1918
War Diary	'M' Camp 27/F 27 C	20/08/1918	22/08/1918
War Diary	Border Camp. 28/A 30 b	23/08/1918	27/08/1918
War Diary	H.Q. Nansens. F.M. 28/B 26.a.75	28/08/1918	30/08/1918
War Diary	H.Q. "O" Camp 28/A 30 d 29	31/08/1918	31/08/1918
Heading	War Diary of 15th Bn. Loyal N Lancs Regt. (Pioneers) From Sept 1st 1918 To Sept. 30th 1918 (Volume IV)		
War Diary	H.Q. at 28/A 30 c. 5.8. Dirty Bucket. A Coy. 1.Z.C. 4.8 (Left) C. Coy. I.Z.d 3.1. (Right) B Coy. B 27. C. 1.3.	01/09/1918	13/09/1918
War Diary	Dirty Bucket 28/A 30 C	14/09/1918	16/09/1918
War Diary	Dominion Camp 28/G 23 d 7.9.	17/09/1918	18/09/1918
War Diary	28/G 23. C. 3.2.	19/09/1918	26/09/1918
War Diary	Duderdom G 30 a 4.0	27/09/1918	28/09/1918
War Diary	Cafe Belge H 29 b 6.9	29/09/1918	30/09/1918
Heading	War Diary 15th Bn Loyal N Lancs Regt (Pioneers) From Oct. 1st 1918 To Oct. 31st 1918 Vol 5		
War Diary	Wytschaete 28/O 19 a 8.8.	01/10/1918	01/10/1918
War Diary	28/T 6 C. 8.8. Wulverghem	02/10/1918	16/10/1918
War Diary	Pont Muhle 28/P 31 b 7.7	17/10/1918	18/10/1918
War Diary	28/W. 8 b. 8.8.	19/10/1918	19/10/1918
War Diary	Tourcoing 28/X 23 a 8.8.	20/10/1918	20/10/1918
War Diary	Estaimpuis 37/B 20 a. 1.8	21/10/1918	31/10/1918
Heading	War Diary Of 15th Bn Loyal N Lancs Regt (Pioneers) From November 1st 1918 To November 30th 1918		
War Diary	Estaimpuis 37/B 20.a.1.8	01/11/1918	15/11/1918
War Diary	Tourcoing 52 Rue St Pierre 36/F 46 3.9.	16/11/1918	19/11/1918
War Diary	Tourcoing F 4b 3.9.	20/11/1918	30/11/1918
Heading	War Diary 15th Bn Loyal N. Lancs Regt From Dec. 1st 1918 To Dec. 31st 1918 Volume VII		

War Diary	Tourcoing F 4 b 3.8	01/12/1918	12/12/1918
War Diary	Tourcoing	13/12/1918	31/01/1919
Heading	War Diary of 15th Bn. Loyal N. Lancs Regt. (Pioneers) From February 1st 1919 To February 28th 1919 (Volume IX)		
War Diary	Tourcoing	01/02/1919	28/02/1919
Heading	War Diary 15th Bn Loyal N. Lancs Regt (Pioneers) From March 1st 1919 To March 31st 1919 Volume X		
War Diary	74 Rue Menin Tourcoing	01/03/1919	09/03/1919
War Diary	34 Rue Amiral Courbet	10/03/1919	14/03/1919
War Diary	Tourcoing	15/03/1919	31/03/1919
Heading	War Diary 15th Bn Loyal N. Lancs Regt. (Pioneers) From January 1st 1919 To January 31st 1919 Volume VIII		
Heading	War Diary 15th Bn Loyal N. Lancs Regt. From April 1st 1919 To April 30th 1919 (Volume XI)		
War Diary	Tourcoing France	01/04/1919	04/04/1919
War Diary	Nechin 37/H 15 b. 5.5.	05/04/1919	30/04/1919
Heading	War Diary 15th Bn. Loyal N. Lancs Regt From May 1st 1919 To May 31st 1919 (Volume XII)		
War Diary	Nechin Belgium	00/05/1919	00/05/1919
Heading	War Diary 15th Bn Loyal N. Lancs Regt From June 1st 1919 To June 15th 1919 (Volume XIII)		
War Diary	Nechin Belgium	01/06/1919	15/06/1919

14TH DIVISION

15TH BN LOYAL NTH LANCASHIRE
(PIONEER BN)
JUN 1918 - JUN 1919

TO FRANCE 1918 JUNE

14TH DIVISION

WAR DIARY

15th Bn LOYAL NORTH LANCS REGT (Pioneers)

From   JUNE 17th 1918

To   JUNE 30th 1918

(Volume I)

June '19

Army Form C. 2118.

WAR DIARY
INTELLIGENCE SUMMARY.
(Erase heading not required.)

Place	Date	Hour	Summary of Events and Information	Remarks and references to Appendices
	JUNE 1918			
TORCY	1.		Warning order to move to AIRE area cancelled. CO's inspection.	JPP
"	2.		Carried on training.	JPP
"	3.		" " " Lt Col S Bingham awarded D.S.O.	JPP
"	4.		Training: Out post schemes by night.	
"	5.		Carried on Training	JPP
"	6.		" " SNCOs flunt to learn reinforcements Batts in pm near AIRE.	
"	7.		" "	
"	8.		Training as above.	JPP
"	9.		No parades.	
"	10.		Training do.	
"	11.		do. CO Carried.	
"	12.		Inspection of Training Staff & Transport by B.G.C.	JPP
"	13.		Training: Orders received 9 pm to move on 14th with by harry.	
"	14.		Training Staff moved in 3 motor lorries via FRUGES - AIRE to NORRENT- FONTES to bric billets rejoining 43rd Inf Bde. HQ. Transport thence	JPP
LAGOULEE	15.		Moved via FRUGES to FIEFS (FIEFS?)	JPP
			Order received 11.45 pm to move by rail from AIRE on 16th with to ENGLAND	
BOULOGNE	16		Left Camp 12.15 pm & marched to entrain at AIRE STATION 2.30 pm reached BOUL OGNE REST CAMP (OSTROHOVE) 12 mn 16/17th.	
BULLSWATER CAMP, SURREY	17		Embarked 11.0 am & crossed to FOLKESTONE, where the Batt. Training Staff entrained; detrained 7.0 pm at BROOKWOOD & marched to Camp at BULLSWATER.	JPP
"	18		Camp; draft arrived Later total of 33 O/R and 357 OR	JPP
"	19		Entire Bn (less arrived 117 OR. Equipment drawn	
"	20		Sundry duties. Batt. officially known as 15th Batt Royal West Kents (Pioneers). Medical inspection. 3 drafts	

WAR DIARY
or
INTELLIGENCE SUMMARY.

(Erase heading not required.)

Army Form C. 2118.

Place	Date	Hour	Summary of Events and Information	Remarks and references to Appendices
BULSWATER CAMP SURREY	20		Further Draft arrived; 423 o.r. Regimental Medical Officer's Medical inspection Adept. Others Ship Adm me ref.	
	21		Strength 2/Br. was 49 offers. 937 o.r. Entire Draft sent to Brigade Guard Room by Br. Trans. Ambulance (Scrub Typhoid Drill). Medical inspection Adept.	R
	22		Surplus officers ordered to return to CROMER. Strength 2/Br. 27 Officers. 993 o.r. Return A.S.B.R. Sqn drill; inoculation.	R
	23		Inoculation. half holiday.	
	24		Form of Punishments; Warning of Thieves (S.1098), fr. C.O. Aldershot. A Coy fires on Bisley Ry.	
	25		Further issues of Equipment & Stores. Musketry; Troop of S.B.R's in Gas	
	26		Battn inspected by Lt. Gen BABTIE. I.M.S. with a view to Medical board for all in fit men. Lieut. Gen. Sir A. Murray Commdg Aldershot Command visited the Camp. Wrote the D.M.O. Strength. 27 offs. 1036 o.r. 69. horses.	
	27		Training by Companies — drill, musketry, P. & B.T. Jns. Strength. 27 off. 1037 o.r. 79 horses.	R
	28		Special Travelling Medical Board visited Battn & saw 300 o.r. of whom they classifies as follows: Class 1. — 1. Class 2. — 43. Class 3 — 242. Class 4. — 23 Strength is now 1 o.r. Training Continues under Company arrangements into the West at BLACKDOWN.	R
	29		Camiss in Training by Companies	
	30		Musketry at Bisley.	R

WAR DIARY

15th Bn. LOYAL NORTH LANCS REGT (Pioneers)

From July 1st 1918
To July 31st 1918

(Volume II)

WAR DIARY or INTELLIGENCE SUMMARY

Army Form C. 2118.

Place	Date July	Hour	Summary of Events and Information	Remarks and references to Appendices
BULLSWATER CAMP	1.		Training under Company arrangements, 2 pm Bn. Route march	H.Q.
PIRBRIGHT	2.		254 OR. found medically unfit, sent away in draft to OSWESTRY	
"	3.		Transport embarks w/c 75 OR. 72 off. left under 2nd Howell by rail from Brookwood at SOUTHAMPTON arriving 5pm. Sailed to HAVRE & proceeded by rail to TERLINKTHUM, just N. of BOULOGNE	H.Q.
"	4.		Training & organization of the Batt. Carried on in Camp. 80 OR. boarded medically unfit. The Batt. left Camp. 10- 10:30pm by rail from BROOKWOOD in 2 parties 2 hours to FOLKESTONE embarked 9am for BOULOGNE. Nominal roll of officers & batallion (Appendix I) marched to OSTROHOVE CAMP on disembarkation	
OSTROHOVE BOULOGNE	5.			
	6.		Left Camp 9.45 am & marched to Shelton, by rail (5 miles) MARQUISE and marched (5 miles) to REBERTINGUE, and HARDINXENT. Transport moved by road from TERLINKTHUM & Iories in the Batt. in the evening. (9 miles) Strength of Batt. off. 34. — 650 OR —	H.Q.
REBERTINGUE	7.		Church Parade. GOC 14th Div. visited the Batt. in billets	H.Q.
"	8.		Drill, Handling of Arms & P.P.R.T. under Company arrangement. Organization of H.Q. Training of Lewis Gunners & Signallers. Carried on	H.Q.
"	9.		Training as above. Lecture by Co. officers on Pioneering & Discipline	
"	10.		Beer. Discipline B? drys Practice land drawn movements. Orders received to move on 12th	H.Q.
"	11.		Training carried on by Companies	
HERBINGHEM	12.		Bn. marched at 10:10 am in 14 Div HQ Group, comprising Transport of Div HQ, Sig HQ, Train HQ, 76 Mot Vet Sect, 14 MG Bn, & 15 L.N.L. under Lt Col S. BINGHAM DSO. HERBINGHEM 9 miles via MESNIL and BOURSIN to billets at Herbinghem	H.Q.

WAR DIARY
or
INTELLIGENCE SUMMARY

Army Form C. 2118.

(Erase heading not required.)

Instructions regarding War Diaries and Intelligence Summaries are contained in F.S. Regs., Part II. and the Staff Manual respectively. Title pages will be prepared in manuscript.

Place	Date JULY	Hour	Summary of Events and Information	Remarks and references to Appendices
MEUQUE	13th		Bn marched at 12.30 pm via LIGNES & TOURNEHEM. Billets in MENTQUE.	HP
—	14th		10 miles. Inspection of billets by Batt comn. and of Troops resting in billet.	HP
—	15th		A Coy on 30th Range. B & C Coy training by Coys. GOC visits the Battn.	HP
—	16th		B. Coy Coy diff coy - C. Company training. A coy at 30 yds range.	HP
—	17th		A Coy with some transport, wearing Box Respirators (Transport by road) to Camp near TERDEGHEM, for work on the WINNEZEELE LINE near X Corps, with CRE 14th Divn. B & C Coys were inspected with 4/3rd Bde Group, on 27 a/P 6 & 6.8, by Gen. Sir H. PLUMER. GCB. GCMG. GCVO. ADC. Commanding Second Army. Draft arrives today. 33 Offrs. 798. OR	HP
—	18th		Training continued. C diff and B Coy company training. 152 OR — strength today.	HP
—	19th		B Coy diff and Coy company training and different a Coy Respr. by Lt Cpl.	HP
—	20th		Training continued. 1 Off. 24 Case developed Scarlet fever.	HP
—	21st		Conference at Divl HQ decided that Quite troops should wear a diff diamond of Yellow, half patches white, half pickelgern in black, a Coy fires on range at NORT BECOURT. 100th gunnery — 200 Officers arrived. RCE Platoon work.	HP
—	22nd		Regimental tug of war Day for B O C reviewed	HP
—	23rd		Drawing continues. House to all offrs by 14 Divl Genl Officer.	HP
—	24th		Oh 2 Companies returning to Battn at EPERLECQUES.	HP
—	25th		Training —missing by heavy rain.	HP
—	26th		— Ditto —. Drawing by Companies in Billets	HP
—	27th		Coi inspection of billets. 1 Rect. Capr GHP REDFORD	HP
—	28th			

WAR DIARY
or
INTELLIGENCE SUMMARY.

Army Form C. 2118.

Place	Date July	Hour	Summary of Events and Information	Remarks and references to Appendices
MENTQUE	29th		B Coy left by march route, staying at LE MARAIS and NOORDPEENE to relieve A Coy on the WINNEZEELE LINE. C Coy digging HQ & Transport firing at 100+ & 200+ range the G.O.C. inspected Transport in the lines at 6.0 pm. C Coy on the range	HP HP
	30th		B Coy arrived in forward area (TERDEGHEM 27 1/40000 / P16 b–5·9), by motor route staging at MENTQUE	HR
	31st		A Coy left forward area to return to Billets at LE MARAIS and NOORDPEENE Since going to the Winnezeele area on July 1st 1918. A Coy carried out during our winter of WINNEZEELE LINE: Training carried on afternoon.	HP

WAR DIARY.

15th Bn Loyal N. Lancs Regt (Pioneers)

From   August 1st 1918.

To   August 31st 1918.

Volume III

WAR DIARY
INTELLIGENCE SUMMARY.

Army Form C. 2118.

(Erase heading not required.)

Place	Date August	Hour	Summary of Events and Information	Remarks and references to Appendices
MENTQUE	1st		No work done - @ Coy to Battn. Strength 34 off. 792 O.R.	HP
" "	2nd		A Coy rejoined Bn at MENTQUE	
" "	3rd		Companies carried on Training. Lecture to Officers on "Intelligence" by GSO III 14 Divr	LPP
" "	4th		Special Report Service for General Gourey, at TERDEGHEM. Battn. was represented by 1 off. & 20 O.R. of C Coy. Declaration given to MOULLE on "Aircraft & Infantry"	HD
" "	5th		14th Division Horse Show	
" "	6th		Carried on training. Draft of 50 O.R. & Lt Hankin returned from Hospital. Strength 35 off. 842.	HO
" "	7th		Company Training A Coy C Coy Pioneer work at T.3.5.d. Beer bombing comes continues	LPP
" "	8th		Battn.	
" "	9th		Training Continued. Conference, demonstration, & discussion in ATTERDEGHEM by Lt. Genl. Sir I. MAXSE Inspector General of Training.	HD
" "	10.		Battn. Sports throughout the day.	
" "	11		12. O.R. of A Coy represented the Battn. at a Special Parade at TERDEGHEM before H.M. THE KING. A Coy differs on the range for Second Army. C. Coy Company Training; B Coy left VILLE in the WINNEZEELE area fly rail to ST MOMELIN.	HD
" "	12			HP
" "	13.		Training carried on. B. Coy reported to Battn.	
" "	14		Training with Special notice to Platoon & Company organisation.	HD
" "	15-		Battn. at Battn.	
" "	16.		Attack practice by C. Coy with RAF cooperation.	
" "	17		Company & Platoon Training. Orders received to move tomorrow.	
LE MARAIS 27a/R2a	18		Battn. marched via MOULLE to LE MARAIS near SERQUES. 6 miles	HR

WAR DIARY or INTELLIGENCE SUMMARY

Army Form C. 2118.

(Erase heading not required.)

Instructions regarding War Diaries and Intelligence Summaries are contained in F. S. Regs., Part II. and the Staff Manual respectively. Title pages will be prepared in manuscript.

Place	Date August	Hour	Summary of Events and Information	Remarks and references to Appendices
LE MARAIS 27a/R2a	19		Batt. remained in billets. Except for a portion of Transport which left by march under 2/Lt Bell via WATTEN to BISSEZEELE. 1 N.C.O. accidentally drowned.	HP
'M' Camp 27/J27c	20		Above Transport concluded march via WORMHOUDT & WATOU, Batt. less other remainder of Transport entrained at STOMER at 8 a.m. detraining PROVEN. Batt. less Transport marched to WATTEN & entrained 10 a.m. detraining PROVEN. Whole Batt. encamped in huts & tents about 27/F27c. M. Camp. 1½ miles West of POPERINGHE.	HP
— —	21		Companies Training under their arrangements.	
— —	22		B. Coy. on Light Railway under 10" C.R.T. in 27/F20. A & C Company Training. Orders received to move forward tomorrow for work.	HP
BORDER CAMP 28/A30.G	23		'A' & 'C' Coys proportion of HQ & Transport moved by march about 1 mile N.W. VLAMERTINGHE for work under II Corps on Shelters on Vlamertinghe–Ypres Railway. HQ. 'B' Coy remained at M. Camp. working on Ypres Railway. (Pyramid) shelters on II Corps work under II Corps. Strength Off. OR. — Draft 9 OR. (B. Coy as for 23rd) 35 =	HP 2/Lt 2/Lt
— —	24		Disposition as on 23rd. — A & C Coys. on work under Vlamedinghe Defence. 2/Lt CASS: returned from Hospital. — B. Coy. Men at Batts. Hrs. now to 4.30pm. Inspection Coys Billets.	2/Lt
— —	25		A & C Coys. on Pyramid Shelters on 24th. Personnel of 11th Batt. The Kings Liverpool Regt. (Cadre Batt) transferred to 7/S. L.N.La.R. with transf. effect from 31.7.15.	2/Lt
— —	26		Rec'd orders to move. B. Coy repairing huts transf. profession round park. A & C Coy on Pyramid Shelters as on 24th. B. Coy Training consol. — also	2/Lt
HQ. NANSENS FM 28/B26.a.7.5	27		Move. — HQ to NANSENS FARM. 28/B 26.a.7.5. 1 mile N.N.W of VLAMERTINGHE. — B. Coy. to MISSION FARM 28/B.27.c.1.3.(Regt) A. Coy to 28/I.2.c.4.8. (miles 4 Bde Bde.) — C. Coy. 28/I.7.d.3.1. (under 43 W Bde)	2/Lt
— —	28		B. Coy. Road tracks in Rpl. area reconstructed. 1 platoon Batt. Officers maintaining above. Remainder improving camp — A. Coy. repairing C.T. 150 CORK LANE & Leuchead front line ??? matchale. — C. Coy. Thickening Repairing Parapets in front line in 28/I.1.16.	2/Lt

A5834 Wt.W4973 M687 750,000 8/16 D. D. & L. Ltd. Forms/C.2118/13.

WAR DIARY
or
INTELLIGENCE SUMMARY

Army Form C. 2118.

(Erase heading not required.)

Place	Date	Hour	Summary of Events and Information	Remarks and references to Appendices
H.Q. NANSEN FARM. 28/B 26 a 7.5.	30.		A.Coy — Day. repairing damage of trench. Repairing trench front wall of parapet, night trekked up 100 x trench for machine gun T.28 N.E. of YPRES. Preparing plank road. C.Coy. erecting walking platform on tracks. Firing shell base. Preparing at Spoilbent material. B.Coy. finishes off parapet of Bay. line front before mentioned.	A.H.
H.Q. "O" camp 28/A 30 d 39	31.		Batt. H.Q. moved to the camp. Continuation of above work. A.Coy. could do little work by day on account of enemy observation. B.Coy. on roads. "O" Coy. on trench or dug outs for R.A.A.	A.H.

WAR DIARY

of

15th Bn LOYAL N LANCS REGT
(Pioneers)

From Sept 1st 1918
To   Sept 30th 1918

(VOLUME IV)

WAR DIARY
INTELLIGENCE SUMMARY

Army Form C. 2118.

Place	Date Sept.	Hour	Summary of Events and Information	Remarks and references to Appendices
HQ at 28/A 30.c.S.8. DIRTY BUCKET A Coy. I.2.c.4.8(hft) C Coy. I.7.d.3.1(R)(pk) B Coy. I3.27.c.13	1		YPRES SECTOR. — One Coy (A) working tfor Bde in the Xrooken Layout Chateaux. A Bde Commun'cation Trenche Party (Body Shield Lt. A.C. Ransdale under Bde in firing line - night B Coy (R.) filled shell hole on front, helping shelter. O.R. slightly wounded, helping guide party.	D.W. D.H.
— 11 —	2		A Coy. & O.R. Continuation as above, also work on dug out. Trenches to firing line. O. Coy. working training Communication	D.H.
— 11 —	3		A Coy. field work 100 Punktags B Coy (R.) on Shafpay Road. C Coy. filled Sandbags & C.T. — New drainage trench up to 1 26 Jun bay — Revitting opening Gds. Some drainage work on dugout — Kash.	D.W.
— 11 —	4		A Coy. building parados 160x hyperhet 4 bys layers of sandbags up. C Coy. 30 Standle Revetting — Sandbags of parapets. — 13.8 Continuation on O.R. work on 340.	J.W.
— 11 —	5		A Revetting in A frames Trench breast work form trench to make damaged by Shells (500 Sandbags laid. @ Coy. Revettings 500 parapet & parados. B Coy: Continuation of work on 3yd.	D.H.
— 11 —	6		A Coy. — 75x Sandbag, 600 Sandbag filled. Laid 24 hundle, erection of banked — carrying C. Coy. — 90 standle earth fee up bused t bunker. R Coy. Repair of Bridge. A splans apron (success) making Good road — Drawing up a before	J.W.
— 11 —	7.8		Companies carried on work as above. Some gas shelling around Coy. HQ: work carried on as above. 1 Casualty. Wounded (A Coy)	
— 11 —	9. 10.		Work as above and in addition a party on repair of light Railway	H.P.
— 11 —	11 12.		Work on same lines but much hindered by weather. B Coy Camp. heavily shelled at KAAIE. No Casualties. work as usual	
— 11 —	13		work as above. Casualties A Coy. 1 K. 1 dof.w. 8 w. all OR.	

WAR DIARY or INTELLIGENCE SUMMARY

Army Form C. 2118.

Place	Date Sept.	Hour	Summary of Events and Information	Remarks and references to Appendices
DIRTY BUCKET 28/A.30.c.	14.		Work by Companies as above. Barrage repairs by B(Res) Coy. LS men YPRES road. Working order received at noon of HP & Res. Coy. on 16s.	HP.
—	15.		Work as above. 41 Bn taking over the whole Div. Front. C. Coy came under them.	
—	16.		A & C. worked as usual. B. Coy moved by march in the morning to camp at G.23.a.7.6. (Sheet 28). Headqrs. even work K.C. Coy.	
DOMINION CAMP 28/G.23.d.7.9.	17		Rt HP & Transport Lines moved by march from DIRTY BUCKET. K DOMINION CAMP. A. Coy moved from KAAIE LINE NORTH of YPRES to DIRTY BUCKET. C. Coy carried on work on roads taken over from B. Coy. B. Coy rested in Camp.	HP
—	18.		A Coy moved to SCOTTISH CAMP. G.23.a.7.6. (sheet 28). B reconnoitred for work on road DICKEBUSCH. CAFE BELGE. VOORMEZEELE. C. Coy carried on their previous work. HP receiving orders for their programme tomorrow.	HP
28/G.23.c.3.2	19.		Batt HQ moved during the day to a farm house at G.23.c.3.2 (500x SE of POPERINGHE) all companies moved in the evening to bivouacs & trenches about MELON COPSE 28/H.26.b. 1500x NW of DICKEBUSCH. Shortly on orders issued from 14 Div. W.E. re(ing) to endeavour to conceal movement of troops, no movement by day, absolute secrecy and urgency of work. B Coy worked on road SE. from CAFE BELGE.	HP
—	20		Small parties by day on road SE from CAFE BELGE 28/H.29 to 8.5. 300 men by night could dump and under Div. Sig. Coy. RE. Reinfcy on roads. 28/H.30.c.3.8. to RAVINE WOOD 28 N.5.G.2.3. Urgently required for guns to move up tonight.	HP
—	21.		C. Coy to shelly wooded road for very urgent work CAFE BELGE to East of VOORMEZEELE on 28/H.30.c. B.3.8 to SCOTTISH WOOD in H.35 b. Casualties B. Coy 1 killed 6 wounded, all OR's.	HP.

WAR DIARY
or
INTELLIGENCE SUMMARY.
(Erase heading not required.)

Army Form C. 2118.

Instructions regarding War Diaries and Intelligence Summaries are contained in F.S. Regs., Part II. and the Staff Manual respectively. Title pages will be prepared in manuscript.

Place	Date Sept.	Hour	Summary of Events and Information	Remarks and references to Appendices
2D/G 13.c.2.2.	22		2 Platoons of each Company working. C. Con ANZAC. H30C.3.8 K VOORMEZEELE (incl.), A. on CAFE BELGE Crater & road behind SCOTTISH WOOD. H35b. B. road in front of ENGLISH WOOD. H30 C. in addition 2 OR killed, mined track from DICKEBUSCH to VOORMEZEELE. Casualties 2 OR wounded. C. Coy.	HP
--	23		Work on roads as above. About 1½ Platoons per Coy. all roads through, & gun [?] in 16 positions further no casualties.	HP
--	24		Work as yesterday patrolling & repairing roads. HP & A Coy billets shelled by 13 cm guns. Casualties 3 OR wounded. (C. Coy & A Coy 2)	HP
--	25		day work on formation of RE Dump at CAFE BELGE (20 men) & Prisoners of War Cage at DICKEBUSCH (25 men); usual road patrols at night.	HP
--	26		Only small road patrols by night to PLUGON per Coy. orders received for HP & move tomorrow to OUDERDOM.	HP
OUDERDOM G.20.a. H.0	27		6 Tool S.C. wagons picked up loads of road timbers from RE Park RUSSEBOOM, & remained loaded in transport lines; no working parties sent out; BaHQ & HQ and Tpt & QM moved to OUDERDOM.	HP
--	28		14th Div attack at 5.30am astride YPRES-COMINES CANAL 16 ST ELOI CRATER & the BLUFF. Companies stood by at HERON COPSE, HK & St. Col Coys RE, ready to go forward on road repair, in two shifts 1st shift, 6 PP Coy; C Coy & ½ B Coy; 2nd Shift - 62nd Tot Coy, A Coy & ½ B Coy. Work repair of VOORMEZEELE - HOLLEBEKE road as top	HP

WAR DIARY or INTELLIGENCE SUMMARY

Army Form C. 2118.

Place	Date Sept	Hour	Summary of Events and Information	Remarks and references to Appendices
DUDERDOM G.20.a.4.0.	28.		forward to bonites. 6GS wagons left lines at 7.0 am to transport road material by far up as possible. 1 pm wagons been up to ST. ELOI rely. team were sent up for at 11.30 pm & work carried on in dark	/P
		8.51 a.m.	1 Platoon of C. Coy went forward, situation being uncertain, to commence road repairs.	
		9.30 a.m.	C Coy & 2 Platoons R Coy went to work on VOORNEZEELE road to form a new MOUND 28/01d. Wagons which brought work by day was not pm. WP coming to ShipyD. This was through too dense traffic, and as good road by noon. Road mines were removed from just west of ST ELOI.	/P
		5 pm	A Coy & 2 Platoons B Coy relieved above shift on the work, where progress with the enemy is putting up very with Trk. Casualties 6 OR. wnds (A.coy) (mds wnds) shrapnel	/P
CAFE BELGE H.29.6.69.	29		Work continues R HULLEBEKE to where point the road was brought for traffic by 5 pm. Bats Hq & 3 Coys moved after work to Hivernage & Huts at H.29.6.69, N/E of DICKEBUSCH.	
-	30.		Work continued on road from ST ELOI via HULLEBEKE to th COMINES CANAL, & made good its whole way. Our Coys working 8.30 am to 2.30 pm. No casualties.	/P

WAR DIARY

15th Bn Loyal N. Lancs Regt (Pioneers)

From Oct. 1st 1918
To   Oct. 31st 1918

Volume V

Army Form C. 2118.

WAR DIARY
or
INTELLIGENCE SUMMARY.
(Erase heading not required.)

Place	Date	Hour	Summary of Events and Information	Remarks and references to Appendices
WYTSCHAETE	OCTOBER 28/10/18		Batt" moved by march via VIERSTRAAT & was rejoined by Pte Batts Transport in Bivouacs about WYTSCHAETE HOSPICE. 24 hour day minimal. Then Coin informs.	
	19.a.8.8. 28+B.2. c.6.8. WULVERGHEM		Batt's moved to Bivouacs + dugouts at M. MIDLAND R.D. & came under XV Corps. fm work East of MESSINES. Transport proceeded via KEMMEL to lines at NEUVE EGLISE. Each Company worked 2 Platoons on roads: WULVERGHEM—MESSINES and WULVERGHEM—PLOEGSTEERT. 2Lts I.HOGG, JT PENDLEBURY, A.THOMPSON, N.G PRICE reported for duty. Coy will run Companies. Some shelling around yesterday.	/AP
	3			AP
	4		Casualty 1 OR wnded. (C. Coy) VIGNACS.	
	5		Work as yesterday. Batt" had leaflets at WULVERGHEM.	AP
	6		Work as above on roads. Twenty three came to me. Following info received for 14 Dur 18.22. "It is unofficially reported that in note addressed by PRINCE MAX of BADEN German Chancellor to President of USA he invites him to ask nations at war to send Plenipotentiaries for the purpose of beginning Peace negotiations and German Government requires that in meantime conclusion of general armistice on land & sea and air be brought about."	AP
	7		Work as before on roads. 2LT A.H BEARD joined for duty following was received 11.35. "There are indications that the attention of Germany is in danger of being diverted by insidious rumours from their single task of defeating the enemy are FM. C. in C. warns all ranks against the old trouble influence of such unfounded peace talk & wishes it to be known there has been a greater need of	

WAR DIARY
INTELLIGENCE SUMMARY.
(Erase heading not required.)

Army Form C. 2118.

Place	Date OCTOBER	Hour	Summary of Events and Information	Remarks and references to Appendices
28/T6 c.8.8.	7		relentless effort & certain promise of great results are the Army will concentrate its entire energy in carrying the operations in West Field to a successful & decisive issue".	HP
WULVERGHEM	8.		Work as above inclusive for MESSINES - WYTSCHAETE Rd. Inspection of Tpt lines by Comdg Officer.	HP
—	9.		Work as above. Transport lines shelled during the evening 2 mules killed & 3 wounded.	HP
—	10.		Work as above. In addition commenced work on road WULVERGHEM - WYTSCHAETE (A Coy). Transport lines moved to new location at 28/T16 C.8.8. Casualties 1 Gnr v. slightly wounded (shrapnel). (C Coy)	HP
—	11.		Work continues as above. A. Wulverghem - Wytschaete Road. B. Wulverghem - Messines road. C. Messines - Kortekeer road.	
—	12.		Work as above.	
—	13.		Work as above. Transport lines & bivouacs shelled for 2½ hrs by Boche H.Q. no casualties.	HP
—	14.		The Second Army continued the attack 14th Divn stood by awaiting results & crossed the LYS RIVER in the afternoon. The Battn stood by in Camp all day.	HP
—	15.		The 14 Divn attacked COMINES at 05:30 & formed a bridgehead. B Coy went out at 12:00 to make good approaches to bridge over the River Lys south of COMINES at 28/V9 & 28. This Company ordered forward. Company at V.1 & 0.9 EUREKA in ex German	HP

C.A.3834 Wt. W.4974/M.687. 750,000 8/16 D.D. & L. Ltd. Forms/C.2118/13.

WAR DIARY
or
INTELLIGENCE SUMMARY.
(Erase heading not required.)

Army Form C. 2118.

Place	Date OCTOBER	Hour	Summary of Events and Information	Remarks and references to Appendices
"28T6C. 8.8 WOLVERGHEM.	1st		Authorities on Platoon of A Coy (2 Lt SHORT MC) went forward to recon. noître & clear sufficiently of enemy traffic the road ESPERANCE CART (0 3 6 b 3.4) – EUREKA (V 1 a 5.7) – SAILORS CROSSING (V 2 b 9.9) & his COMINES. All roads were in very good condition. This Platoon too bivacked in old German Dump about V 2 b 7.8. Lt F.R. VIPOND joined for duty. Casualties Nil.	HP
"	16.		A Coy working on road as yesterday. B Coys Bridge approaches. 'C' Coy moved up to bivouacs about 28/V 1 d 4.4. & coy machines in Camp all day.	HP.
PONT AVHLE 28/P31 b 7.7	17		A & B working on Bridge approaches over the LYS V 4 d 0.9 and V 9 b 3.8. C Coy to work on COMINES road & moved to bivouacs in COMINES area move to P 31 b 7.7 am) P 31 d 3.7. Batt HQ & Transport lines moved to 0 3 6 d 7.7) during the day.	k
"	18		Work as yesterday on Bridge approaches. & MESSINES – COMINES road. A Coy on Bridge approaches remainder on road COMINES – WERVICQ SUD – LINSELLES Dump. B Coy companies attend prepared (moving)	HP
M/8/35 8.8	19 20		K area PAPT BUCQ LA MONTAGNE 28/W.2 and B Transport lines moved to P 31 a 4.5.	HP.
TOURCOING. 28/X 2.2 a 8.8 ESTAMPUIS. 37/B 2.0 a.1.8	20 21		Transport rejoined the Bn. Bn Batt marched an 13.00 via LE BLATON – BLANC FOUR – N outskirts of TOURCOING to billets at VIELLE MOTTE Batt marched 11.00 via WATTRELOS to billets in ESTAMPUIS. Advance parties were sent forward to reconnoitre roads & Buttonal area about DOTTIGNIES, for work.	HP

Army Form C. 2118.

WAR DIARY
or
INTELLIGENCE SUMMARY.
(Erase heading not required.)

Instructions regarding War Diaries and Intelligence Summaries are contained in F. S. Regs., Part II. and the Staff Manual respectively. Title pages will be prepared in manuscript.

Place	Date	Hour	Summary of Events and Information	Remarks and references to Appendices
ESTAIMPUIS	22 OCTOBER		Bn't remained in billets; reconnoitring parties sent out; Ch. & Section per Coy, onto roads in Bn Divisional area East of DOTTIGNIES.	1/H
27/B Coy 1.8			in artm. Company training carried out :—	
"	23		"	2H
"	24		by known escort O.W. Patrol. (about 1 Off & 20 O.R.) from Coys on	2H
"	25		" a road repairs.	2H
"	26		"	2H
"	27		Bn moved took over new area on night 27/28. Sent out a party to reconnoitre new roads to in their area.	2H
"	28		Coys carried out training — Hoy escort on road repairs battalion baked.	2H
"	29		Bathing Coy repairing Railway sidings and a draft attack scheme.	1H
"	30		but training carried out. Coys Railway Repairs from Coys Patrols above	1H
"	31		by Enemy carried out. Patrols 29/7. 29 Remainder did not move. At 16 hrs. moved to DOTTIGNIES & Leaving A boy located in Leaving	2H

WAR DIARY

OF

15TH Bn LOYAL N. LANCS REGT (Pioneers)

From   November 1st 1918
To   November 30th 1918

(VOLUME VI)

WAR DIARY
or
INTELLIGENCE SUMMARY.
(Erase heading not required.)

Army Form C. 2118.

Place	Date	Hour	Summary of Events and Information	Remarks and references to Appendices
ESTAIMPUIS 37/B20.a.1.8.	Nov. 1		A "B" Coy. at DOTTIGNIES. Flying shell hole - made footbridge re (36 ORs). Patrol (20 OR.) filled in shell hole on road. Coy training. Patrol on road.	2N
"	2		Training carried on. Road patrolled.	2N
"	3		Do. — do. —	2N
"	4		Do. — do. — Road patrolled — road improved to Attiches	2N
"	5		Do. — Clear roads in DOTTIGNIES. Road patrolled. 25 OR making approach to position. Training carried on. Pan. l 40th Div. area taken over — Road bridge over ESCAUT.	2N
"	6		Do — do. — Pan. l 40th Div. area taken over 60 OR. filled in shell holes	2N
"	7		reconnoitred. 3 Road patrols about 7 OR's wounded	2N
"	8		Training carried on. Road patrolled, repaired, cleared.	2N
"	9		No — do — Roads patrolled. 1 Company carried planks to approach to new Bridge across ESCAUT at C. St. 37. E Coy moved from 37/B20.a.1.8. to 29/4.29.c.5.2. — on arrival worked from 8pm on approach to bridge at C.S. A 3.7. L Coy making plank road to INGLIS BRIDGE. 110 yds completed. — 190 Yds formation ready for planking.	2N
"	10		180 yds of plank road completed — road now completed with exception of 2 sharp curves, unable to complete until INGLIS Bdge finished. Loading, unloading, carrying timber, filling in shell holes. Improved ramp approach to Pontoon bridge.	2N

Army Form C. 2118.

WAR DIARY
or
INTELLIGENCE SUMMARY.
(Erase heading not required.)

Instructions regarding War Diaries and Intelligence Summaries are contained in F.S. Regs., Part II. and the Staff Manual respectively. Title pages will be prepared in manuscript.

Place	Date	Hour	Summary of Events and Information	Remarks and references to Appendices
ETAIMPUIS 37/B.20.a.1.8.	Nov 11		Armistice signed with Germany. This however did not affect the Batt's work making switch road to flank road. 20 yds. completed. Timber lorries unloaded. Rouling R.E.'s to get the bridge across river.	J.W.
	12		40 yds flank road switch made – switch completed.	J.W.
	13		40 yds Western slit earth – ramp to new approach to INGUL'S Bridge. Building up Main N side of ramp (under 610th Field Coy R.E.) also making brick also loading at R.E. dump.	J.W.
	14		Unloading lorries. C Coy moved from 29/U.29.C.5.2. to 37/B.20.a.1.8. by buses after work on France Leaving to Bridge. A & B Coys continued work in shifts.	Ho
	15		Coys at disposal of O's C. Coys Conference of O.C Coy to determine Policy to be followed regarding Educational Scheme.	
TOURCOING 52 Rue St Pierre 36/F.4.b.3.9.	16		Batt'n moved by trans't to TOURCOING via PETIT. AUDENARDE & WATTRELOS & concentrated in billets.	
	17		Coys at disposal of O.C Coys. Batt'n representative at Thanksgiving Parades at ROUBAIX & TOURCOING. Con Training but a series of inspection by Corps Commander.	
	18			
	19		Con Training: Dr W. Frost Agricultural Employment formed, consisting of HQ Batt, RA, & Pioneers, & attached to the Batt.	

Army Form C. 2118.

WAR DIARY
or
INTELLIGENCE SUMMARY.
(Erase heading not required.)

Instructions regarding War Diaries and Intelligence Summaries are contained in F. S. Regs., Part II. and the Staff Manual respectively. Title pages will be prepared in manuscript.

Place	Date Nov	Hour	Summary of Events and Information	Remarks and references to Appendices
TOURCOING F4 b 39	20		Special Demobilisation forms for Miners & Railway Personnel Issued. Lecture in CINEMA, by 2 Lt STEVENS, 1st LWC, on Demobilisation & Reconstruction - attended by the whole Batt.	JP
	21		Corps prectices for Inspection by Corps Commander - 20 men leaving tonight.	
	22		Coy Drill as yesterday, 20 men leaving tonight. Cattle lorries changed about.	JP
	23		Batt. Dining Hall formed for Officer ranks including 9 Non Corporal. Batt. Drill, rehearsal & March Past.	
	24		Church Parade. - 09-30.	
	25		Batt. Parade - rehearsal of March Past for 2nd & 5th inst. Inspection by Corps Commander Cancelled. Inspection of Billets by Commanding Officer.	JP
	26			
	27		Inspection of Transport by Commanding Officer.	JP
	28		Batt. Drill - rehearsal for Corps Commander's Parade tomorrow. Companies at disposal of O.C. Coys.	JP
	29		14 Divl. Troops. (Div Auth - 16th Lancers - 14 Bde M.G.C.) Inspected by XV Corps Commander at Genl. Sir Beauvoir de Lisle, on 36.7.25 & 8.8 near MOUVEAUX. The Batt. moved past by companies in column.	JP
	30			

WAR DIARY

15th Bn LOYAL N. LANCS REGT

FROM Dec 1st 1918
TO Dec 31st 1918

Volume VII.

Army Form C. 2118.

WAR DIARY
or
INTELLIGENCE SUMMARY.
(Erase heading not required.)

Instructions regarding War Diaries and Intelligence Summaries are contained in F.S. Regs., Part II. and the Staff Manual respectively. Title pages will be prepared in manuscript.

Place	Date	Hour	Summary of Events and Information	Remarks and references to Appendices
TOURCOING F4 b 38	DECEMBER			
	1st		Church Parade at the Municipal Theatre. 10.00 the Baths by Companies. Agricultural Coy. working at WATTRELOS.	H.P.
	2nd		Corps. arm'd disposal of O's C. Corps. 14 Div. Torch light Tattoo in the GRAND PLACE, ROUBAIX 18.30. at which the Bn. Band was represented.	H.P.
	3rd			
	4th		Batt. Parade, rehearsal for preliminary inspection by 27th Army Commander; Div Troops Agricultural Coy moved to WATTRELOS by motor.	
	5th		Company under O.C. Batt. played Second round of WITH queen 2 - 0.	H.P.
	6th		Batt. Paraded at 11.00 at MOUVEAUX on 14 Div. Parade in rehearsal for inspection near week by Army Commander.	
			Commanding Officer inspected billets in the morning. H.M. THE KING visited 1st XV Corps area.	
	7th		Church Parade 11.00 at Municipal Theatre.	
	8th		Competition in Dispatch of O.C. Coys. 14 Div. Torch light Tattoo in GRAND PLACE TOURCOING. 18.00	H.P.
	9th			
	10th		Div. Band at MOUVEAUX for inspection by the XV Corps Comdr.	H.P.
	11th		Coys at disposal of O.C. Coys. 6 miniers sent to Corps Glouc- ester Station; LA MADELEINE for release for coal mining at home	H.P.
	12th		G. O. C. 14 Div. visited all Batt. billets - 7 miniers released for coal mining at home	H.P.

Army Form C. 2118.

WAR DIARY
or
INTELLIGENCE SUMMARY.
(Erase heading not required.)

Instructions regarding War Diaries and Intelligence Summaries are contained in F. S. Regs., Part II. and the Staff Manual respectively. Title pages will be prepared in manuscript.

Place	Date	Hour	Summary of Events and Information	Remarks and references to Appendices
TOURCOING	13		Lect. on Demobilization to 14 Dis. by Rev. Stadon Kennedy, M.C., C.F.	/AP
	14		10 miners despatched for release. Infantry at disposal of O.C. Corps. 16 miners despatched for release	
	15		Church Parade 11:00 at Municipal Theatre.	/AP
	16		4 miners despatched for Release.	
	17		4 miners despatched for Release.	
	18		Lect. to Batt. on Demobilization by Lt. Thompson. B.S. Education Officer. The last Seven miners despatched for release. The G.O.C. visited the Batt. to present a wreath to the widow of the Dux Croix Coutria Race.	
	19		Companies at the disposal of O.C. Corps. Rout marching & Inspections. Same as yesterday. The Batt. played La Friand running LE Duc Football	/AP
	20		League v. R.A.M.C. & Lon 4-0.	
	21		Draft received from the Base. 31 O.R.	
	22nd		Church Parade 11:00 hr. at Municipal Theatre.	/AP
	23rd		Companies at Disposal of O.C. Corps - Educational Classes.	
	24th		Same as above.	
	25th		No Parades.	/AP
	26th		Parades under Company arrangement. Educational Classes.	
	27		Same as above.	
	28		Same as above.	
	29		Church Parade Municipal Theatre.	
	30		Route march by Companies. Educational Classes.	
	31		N.C.Os despatched for Release for Long Service	/AP

Army Form C. 2118.

WAR DIARY
or
INTELLIGENCE SUMMARY.
(Erase heading not required.)

Instructions regarding War Diaries and Intelligence Summaries are contained in F. S. Regs., Part II. and the Staff Manual respectively. Title pages will be prepared in manuscript.

Place	Date	Hour	Summary of Events and Information	Remarks and references to Appendices
TOURCOING	January 1919	1	Parades under Company arrangements. Recreation Classes.	
	2		Batt. inspected by G.O.C. 14. Div. A. Coy. to Lilleton Regt. full marching order.	H.P.
			E. Coy. Company Organisation – 2 OR dispatched for release on Reg. Soldier.	
	3rd		Companies at Disposal of O.C. Coy.	H.P.
	4th		Companies at Disposal of O.C. Coy.	
	5th		Church Parade at Municipal Theatre. 4 OR dispatched for Release as slip	H.P.
			men. 1 for Kent Review.	
	6th		Companies at the disposal of O.C. Corps.	
	7th		Lecture given by Sen. Off. to Line Runs. on British System. & Daughterlers relations (Capt R.E. Chadwyck)	H.P.
	8th		Company Parades. Sold in dispatched.	H.P.
			1 Regular	
			2 Pivotal men dispatched.	
	9th		Lecture by Educ. Off. to B. Coy. remainder on Company Parades 1 Pivotal man also dispatched.	H.P.
	10th		Company Parades under O.C. Coy.	H.P.
	11th		24 Hours + 4 other ranks dispatched for dispersal. Company Parades.	
	12th		3 OR dispatched for release. 1 Off. and 23 OR sent to form American Staging	H.P.
			Camp. Tourcoing in connection with Demobilization of Americans.	
	13th		6 OR dispatched for release. Batt. Sports held morning & afternoon.	H.P.
	14th		Parades in the Company any arrangements.	
	15th		Lecture to Batt. by Educ. Off. on "Czecho-Slovaks."	H.P.

Army Form C. 2118.

WAR DIARY
or
INTELLIGENCE SUMMARY.

(Erase heading not required.)

Instructions regarding War Diaries and Intelligence Summaries are contained in F.S. Regs., Part II. and the Staff Manual respectively. Title pages will be prepared in manuscript.

Place	Date	Hour	Summary of Events and Information	Remarks and references to Appendices
TOURCOING	16th		Company Parade under arrangements of O.C. Coy. Rest arranged for Bath.	AP
	17th		17 OR despatched for Relieve.	
	18th		Church Parade at Municipal Theatre. 19 OR despatched for Relieve.	AP
	19th		2Lt F.R. Vipond detached to Pivates.	
	20th		Parade under Company arrangements. 18 OR despatched for Relieve.	AP
	21st		8 OR despatched for Relieve.	
	22nd		Rehearsal Parade for Presentation of Colour. on Sat 25th 19 OPP despatched for Relieve.	AP
	23rd		Parades under Company arrangements.	
	24th		Rehearsal Parade for Presentation of Colour. 13 OR despatched for Relieve.	
	25th		The Battalion was Presented, by Lt. Gen. Sir BEAUVOIR DE LISLE, Commdg XV Corps, in the GRANDE PLACE ROUBAIX, with a Colour given by HIS MAJESTY KING GEORGE V, in memory of the Batt: An Escort was reported to Pepenceh Lt. the memory of the Colour under CAPT A.G.H. DEAN by 2 Lt BEARD (Ensign) CSM's LLOYD and Mc. DEAN and CAPT FLOOD and (Colour Guard) 1 Platoon. Colour Escort under Lt ATTWOOD & 2Lt PENDLEBURY. After concentration & Presentation of the Colour the Parade marched past, & returned to Quarters, where the Colour was received	AP

Army Form C. 2118.

WAR DIARY
or
INTELLIGENCE SUMMARY.
(Erase heading not required.)

Instructions regarding War Diaries and Intelligence Summaries are contained in F. S. Regs., Part II. and the Staff Manual respectively. Title pages will be prepared in manuscript.

Place	Date	Hour	Summary of Events and Information	Remarks and references to Appendices
JOUREUX	Jan 25		by the Batt Guard, & by a guard of 3 Platoons at the Men.	AP.
"	26		14. OR. Sent for Dispersal. Church Parade.	
"	27		17. OR. Sent for Dispersal. Parades by Companies	WS
"	28		19. OR. Sent for Dispersal. 9 Officers. 2Lt. BEARD & 2Lt. CLAYTON.	
"	29		21 OR. Sent for Dispersal. In Div Troops Reg'tl. Company were the Guards & returned to Units less k the Bakers by the Senr. Officers on "Colonial" Government.	WP.
"	30		Parades under Company arrangements	
"	31		Inspection of Billets by Commanding Officer — 14.00 hrs Lecture by Canadian Officer to the Batt on the Colours, on the Colours in the Crown War on Parade.	AP

Vol 9

WAR DIARY
of
15th Bn LOYAL N LANCS REGT
(Pioneers)

From February 1st 1919
To   February 28th 1919

(VOLUME IX)

WAR DIARY
or
INTELLIGENCE SUMMARY.
(Erase heading not required.)

Army Form C. 2118.

Instructions regarding War Diaries and Intelligence Summaries are contained in F. S. Regs., Part II. and the Staff Manual respectively. Title pages will be prepared in manuscript.

Place	Date	Hour	Summary of Events and Information	Remarks and references to Appendices
TOURCOING	February 1st		20. OR. Sent for Dispersal. Coy Officers inspected Companies in billets.	WP.
	2nd		13. OR. Sent for Dispersal. Church Parade on Municipal Theatre.	
	3rd		18. OR. Sent for Dispersal. Parades & Educational Classes now on.	
	4th		Parades by Companies. Coy Officers inspected C. Coy in billets.	JHP
	5th		Education Officer lectures to Bahn on the new Scheme for the formation of the Army of Occupation & its effect on Demobilization.	
	6th		25 OR. sent for dispersal. Also Lt. HOLDSWORTH & 2Lt. TONG.	HP.
	7th		Owing to reduction of numbers the Bahn was reorganized into R: HQ Transport & one Company (Z) under Major SIR Thomas. The Company consisting of 3 Platoons A, B, & C. The remainder of the above Companies. The Bahn was concentrated after Bahn HQ moved to 74, Rue de MENIN. TOURCOING. 14. OR Sent for Dispersal.	HP.
	8th		12. O.R. sent for Dispersal.	
	9th		14. OR sent for dispersal. Parades under Coy arrangements.	HP
	10th		36. OR. sent for Normal.	
	11th		Parade was Coy arrangements. Coy Officers inspected billets.	HP
	12th		Lect. to Bahn by Educ. Officer - Subject "The Franchise".	
	13th		48. OR. Sent for Dispersal.	
	14th		29. OR. Sent for Dispersal. Allotment made out up to 16 £.	

Army Form C. 2118.

WAR DIARY
or
INTELLIGENCE SUMMARY.
(Erase heading not required.)

Instructions regarding War Diaries and Intelligence Summaries are contained in F.S. Regs., Part II. and the Staff Manual respectively. Title pages will be prepared in manuscript.

Place	Date	Hour	Summary of Events and Information	Remarks and references to Appendices
TOURCOING	9.14		Billetin with leave to Bath in town dress. Conferences of 4 O.R. released — 43 O.R. Cadres, 209 O.R. to the Armys occupation to keep him orderly to organise their personnel as a Syndicate for Training Purposes on the lines of a School.	1/2
	15th		12. O.R. sent for Dispersal.	1/2
	16th		9. O.R. sent for Dispersal. Church Parade or Municipal Theatre.	1/2
	17th		Parade under Company arrangements. It was not found possible to continue Training as intended on 14th with owing to depletion of personnel + numbers of fatigues.	
	18th		An attempt was made to provide an Syndicate for Training Purposes but this was not found feasible.	1/2
	19th		Owing to breakdown of Div. Baths, May were apparently under Batt. arrangements. 3. O.R. sent for Dispersal. 1 Strong (Capt. HARKERS) + (3) O.R. sent as Guard to Supply train at ST ANDRÉ.	1/2
	20th		Parades under Coy. Pay and interest.	
	21st		Short leaven given to Representation of ½ people. concession was continued attain.	1/2
	22nd		A.C.1s + on Quot. Prisoners under Company arrangements.	1/2
	23rd		Church Parade or Municipal Theatre.	
	24th		Parades under Company arrangements.	1/2

Army Form C. 2118.

WAR DIARY
or
INTELLIGENCE SUMMARY.
(Erase heading not required.)

Instructions regarding War Diaries and Intelligence Summaries are contained in F. S. Regs., Part II. and the Staff Manual respectively. Title pages will be prepared in manuscript.

Place	Date	Hour	Summary of Events and Information	Remarks and references to Appendices
TOURCOING	Feb 25		Parades with Company arrangement	U.P
	26		as above. Comdg Officer inspected billets.	
	27		as above. Kit inspection.	V.P
	28		Baths under Batt. arrangements.	

WAR DIARY

15th Bn LOYAL N. LANCS REGT
(Pioneers)

FROM MARCH 1st 1919

TO MARCH 31st 1919

VOLUME X

Army Form C. 2118.

WAR DIARY
or
INTELLIGENCE SUMMARY.
(Erase heading not required.)

MARCH 1919.

Instructions regarding War Diaries and Intelligence Summaries are contained in F. S. Regs., Part II. and the Staff Manual respectively. Title pages will be prepared in manuscript.

Place	Date	Hour	Summary of Events and Information	Remarks and references to Appendices
74 Rue MENIN TOURCOING	1.		Batt. Employed on fatigues.	
	2.		Church Parade at Municipal Theatre.	
	3.		Capt HARKNESS + 20 O.R. Supply Sword Bayonets from HAZEBROUCK.	N.P.
	4.		Total hours worked bdak. 14. fore no. 4 tr 3yrs. 12. tr 24 yrs.	
	5.		Parade under Company arrangements. Orders received to form Cadre A. in shape of Cadre B. i.e. with no animals; 85 bayts & armourers & all. 34. all clerks.	N.P.
	6.		Owing to reduction of animals, orders received to tram past platoon as soon as possible & NECHIN. Very to entrainment. 3 cookers & 2 water carts sent today with a guard.	N.P.
	7.		Brigade Officers entrusted to examine 81st & 82nd Coys. (A.F. S.1098) 5 S. Wagons & tools embarked to NECHIN.	N.P.
	8.		Sent to Base for duty. 5 S. hitchin with first Genl. Saddling stores despatched to NECHIN. Armourers Blues down also by O.C. Clearing Officer;	N.P.
	9.			N.P.
34 RUE AMIRAL COURBET	10.		17 OR sent to dispersal. 2nd Lt JAMES on draft conducting duty; proceeded from NECHIN to billets in Rue AMIRAL COURBET No.s 22, 34, 36, TOURCOING. The Batt moved to billets in Rue AMIRAL COURBET Nos 22, 34, 36, TOURCOING.	N.P.
	11.		Batt. employed in billets; 5. Lt Draft Home despatched & Knotlice Camp	N.P.
	12.		Parade under Company arrangements.	
	13.		Parade under Company arrangements. Colours were transferred to NECHIN, & placed in charge of 2nd Lt D.S. WILSON	N.P.

Army Form C. 2118

WAR DIARY
or
INTELLIGENCE SUMMARY.
(Erase heading not required.)

Instructions regarding War Diaries and Intelligence Summaries are contained in F.S. Regs., Part II. and the Staff Manual respectively. Title pages will be prepared in manuscript.

Place	Date March 1919	Hour	Summary of Events and Information	Remarks and references to Appendices
TOURCOING	15		Capt. Maunsell, Flood, Hawkes, Lt Johnson, 246 Cor., Hogg, Pendler arr. Remittance to 12.LNL; Lt N.Lane, to volunteers for Army of Occupation.	1HP
	16		Church Parade at Church Army Hut. TOURCOING.	1HP
	17		Parade under Company arrangement	1HP
	18		Company Parade; 2.LD Horses despatched to TOURCOING CAMP.	1HP
	19		Company Rank March; Lts. Badger, Muckleston, Gibson & 2 Lr. Dunkley reported for duty from 12. Konyar N.Lives.	
	20		B.O.C Parade at HERSEAUX.	
	21		Details & 14 Rt M/C attached to R Batt: (12 off. 178 OR) tin cadre having proceeded to UK.	1HP
	22		2.LD horses sent to TOURCOING Camp, learning an attempt 8 wards; Battalion Have + Hands in not manned. All leave & Demobilization stopped owing to Railway Strikes in England.	1HP
	23		Lt Allen joined for duty from 12.LNL Company Parades.	1HP
	24		Parade under Company arrangements	
	25		Normal railway traffic resumed. Company Parades	
	26		Parade under Company arrangements	1HP
	27		140 OR. MG Details despatched (officer (Major Q.I.R Hams) sent for dispersal (Capt Hallam, disbanded	
	28		42 OR. Sent 15 Y/5 KORL at BRUSSELS 8 officers & 60 OR sent for dispersal; 8 officers & 60 OR sent for dispersal	
	29		Lt Taylor, Lt Badger, Gibson. all orr.)	
	30		40 OR. Sent K. Y/5 KORL	
	31		41 OR. Sent K. Y/5 KORL; 3 off. + 7 OR sent for dispersal Lt Attwood, Muckleston, 2Lr Dunkley OR. 55. + 4 Horses	1HP
			Batt: returned to Cajun 8h 14 bk attached; Strength 5 ft 15	

WAR DIARY

15th Bn LOYAL N. LANCS REGT (Pioneers)

FROM JANUARY 1st 1919

TO JANUARY 31st 1919

VOLUME VIII

Vol. 11

WAR DIARY

15th Bn LOYAL N. LANCS REGT

From April 1st 1919
To April 30th 1919

(Volume XI)

Army Form C. 2118.

WAR DIARY
or
INTELLIGENCE SUMMARY.
(Erase heading not required.)

1st K.N.Regt. APRIL 1919.

Instructions regarding War Diaries and Intelligence Summaries are contained in F. S. Regs., Part II. and the Staff Manual respectively. Title pages will be prepared in manuscript.

Place	Date April	Hour	Summary of Events and Information	Remarks and references to Appendices
TOURCOING FRANCE	1st		Collection & Stores organization of Cadre on return.	
	2nd		2 OR. despatched to 1/5 KORL.	
	2nd		1 Officer (2Lt F.T. STEVENS) & 1 OR sent for Dispersal	
	4th			
NECHIN. 27/H15.6 S.S.	5th		Cadre moved to LILLE at NECHIN. by train. 9 (nine) K. Batt: Stores concentrated for ent[r]ainment	
	6th		Inspection of LILLE.	
	7th		4 OR F/S KORL Germany.	
	8th		Remains in LILLE.	
	9th			AP
	10th			
	11th/12th		Capt P.V. DAVIES took over duties of Staff Capt. Courtrai Area H.S. Remains in LILLE. KORL. & Officer & 85 other[s]	AP
	13th		others returned for Educational Course in England.	AP
	14th		Lt R. MORE despatched for Dispersal.	
	15th		Lt J. Atkinson departs for Dispersal. Lt Col S. Poulton took over command of Cadre	AP
	16th		14 Dr Pickett - Capt H. Fifrin[?] Remained in LILLE.	
	17th		Leave allotment to Cadre.	AP
	18th		1 OR. sent to Demobilization	AP
	19th		2 OR sent for Dispersal. Leave now to Cadre on reason	AP
			for retention is that country states of returning home by July	
Tue 30th			Remained in LILLE. No event of any sort to record.	RS

WAR DIARY

15th Bn LOYAL N. LANCS REGT

From   May 1st 1919

To   May 31st 1919.

(VOLUME XII)

Army Form C. 2118.

WAR DIARY
or
INTELLIGENCE SUMMARY.
(Erase heading not required.)

Place	Date	Hour	Summary of Events and Information	Remarks and references to Appendices
NECHIN, BELGIUM	MAY 1919.		During this month Hr Cadre remained in Net down billets, Guard of Equipment on may 9th. The Cadre was reduced by 2. OR. & a Serjeant & 36. OR. on may 16th. an Equipment was inspected by Hr Corps. Inspecting Ordnance Officer. On May 19th the Officer (CAPT W.S. TAYLOR) proceeded to U.K. for Repatriation to INDIA. Throughout the month, no event of importance occurred.	Jer.

WAR DIARY

15th Bn Loyal N Lancs Regt

From June 1st 1919
To June 15th 1919

(Volume XIII)

WAR DIARY
or
INTELLIGENCE SUMMARY.

Army Form C. 2118.

June 1919

Place	Date	Hour	Summary of Events and Information	Remarks and references to Appendices
Nechin BELGIUM	1st		Preparations made for reduction of Cadre to 2 Off & 10 O.R. the rest to be released. All stores off loaded from wagons into Store.	HP
	2nd		Orders received for Cadre to proceed home by ST ANDRE and BOULOGNE on 14th inst. Leaving all equipment with a guard of 2 off & 10 O.R. known as "Equipment Guard"	HP
	11th		Orders received for Equipment Guard to entrain with Equipment at NECHIN on 16th inst.	HP
	12th		Vehicles loaded, checked, & inventoried, wagons & packages marked 15 LNL, E 352, RE HUTS, BLACKDOWN (their serial numbering & Destination).	HP
	12th		as above 12th	
	14th		Cadre, with Colour in charge of 2 Lt Jones left by train at 9.45 hours for St ANDRE, LILLE	HP
	16th		Vehicles moved to NECHIN Station in preparation for entrainment at 9.00 hours for 16th for U.K. via ANTWERP.	

[signature] Major
O. i/c DG. 15th Bn. LOYAL NORTH LANCASHIRE REGT.

www.ingramcontent.com/pod-product-compliance
Lightning Source LLC
Chambersburg PA
CBHW081455160426
43193CB00013B/2491